ECUADOR

DISCOVER ECUADOR CULTURE, SPORTS, HISTORY, CUISINE, LANDMARKS, PEOPLE, TRADITIONS, AND MANY MORE FOR KIDS

LOCATION

North - Borders with Colombia

West - Pacific Ocean

East- Borders with Brazil and Peru

South - Borders with Peru

POPULATION

17 million

China population
1425 Millions

India Population
1428 Millions

CLIMATE

Temperate maritime climate

Wet season

December and May

Dry season

June to November

INDEPENDENCE

August 10th, 1809

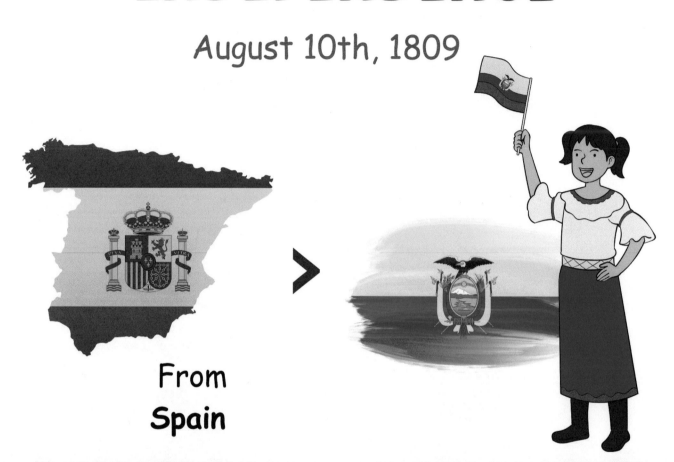

From
Spain

MOTTO > "Dios, patria y libertad" means "God, homeland, and liberty"

CAPITAL

Quito

- Quito is one of the highest capital cities in the world

- It is famous for its well-preserved colonial architecture.

- The equator line, from which the country gets its name, is just a short drive away

- Quito is surrounded by beautiful mountains, offering great views and outdoor activities

- The historic center of Quito is a UNESCO World Heritage Site

CURRENCY

US Dollar (USD)

Denominations notes

$1, $5, $10, $20, $50, $100

Coins - 1,5,10,25,50 Cents

EDUCATION

Education is free and compulsory from ages 5 to 14

Includes primary, Middle and high schooling.

LANGUAGE

Official
Language

NATIONAL FLAG

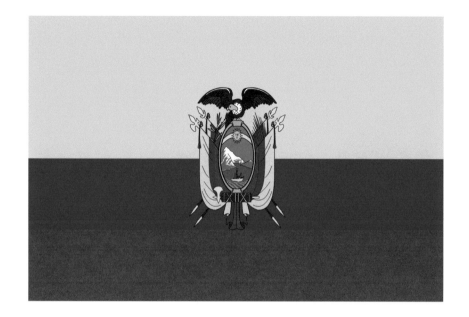

- Yellow shows the country's wealth and resources

- Blue symbolizes the clear skies and clear waters of Ecuador

- Red represents the blood shed by the heroes

NATIONAL ANIMAL

Andean Condor

- The Andean Condor is one of the largest flying birds in the world.

- It is a symbol of power and freedom in Ecuadorian culture.

- It found in the Andes Mountains, it soars gracefully through the skies.

- Andean Condors have a distinctive white collar of feathers around their necks.

- They are scavengers, feeding mainly on carrion.

NATIONAL BIRD

Andean Cock-of-the-Rock

- The Andean Cock-of-the-Rock is known for its bright orange plumage.

- It is found in cloud forests of the Andes.

- Males perform elaborate courtship displays to attract females.

- Their diet consists mainly of fruits and insects.

- They are considered a symbol of beauty and vitality.

NATIONAL FLOWER

Rose

- Ecuador is famous for its high-quality roses, which are exported worldwide.

- Roses come in various colors and are grown in the Andean highlands.

- Ecuadorian roses are prized for their large blooms and long stems.

- The rose industry is an important part of Ecuador's economy.

- Roses symbolize love, beauty, and friendship.

NATIONAL TREE

Cinchona Tree

- Cinchona trees are native to the Andes and are known for their medicinal properties

- The bark of the Cinchona tree contains quinine, used to treat malaria.

- Cinchona trees are often found in cloud forests.

- It has small, white or pink flowers and glossy green leaves.

- The tree is named after the Countess of Chinchón, who popularized the use of quinine.

TRADITIONAL MEDICINE

1) Chamomile

- Used to treat digestive issues such as indigestion, bloating, and stomach cramps.

2) Sarsaparilla

- Used to support kidney and liver health

3) Valerian

- It is often used as a sleep aid to improve sleep quality and treat insomnia.

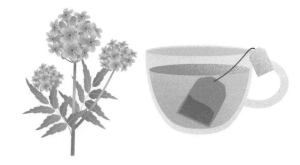

4) Cat's Claw

- This vine is used to boost the immune system and reduce inflammation.

THE GALAPAGOS ISLANDS

- The Galapagos Islands are home to some of the most unique and fascinating animals in the world!

- Can see giant tortoises, marine iguanas, blue-footed boobies, and even penguins, all of which can't be found anywhere else on Earth.

- The Galapagos Islands were formed by volcanic activity millions of years ago

- People can explore the rugged landscapes, walk on lava fields, and even see active volcanoes! It's like stepping into another world full of adventure and mystery.

MAJOR NATIONAL PARKS

There are 11 National Parks in Ecuador

Galapagos > Cajas > Yasuni

Sangay > Cotopaxi

LAND MARKS

Otavalo Market

El Panecillo

TelefériQo

Los Frailes Beach

Mindo Cloud Forest

Cuicocha Crater Lake

LAND MARKS

Galapagos Islands

Mitad del Mundo

Cotopaxi Volcano

Ingapirca

Avenue of the Volcanoes

Quito's Historic Center

EXPORTS

Oil

Bananas

Seafood

Cocoa

Flowers

Shrimp

ECONOMY
Based on

Oil

Manufacturing

Mining
(gold, silver)

Shrimp Farming

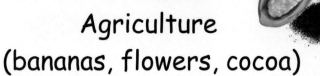

Agriculture
(bananas, flowers, cocoa)

Tourism

MARINE LIFE

Eco system most diverse in the world

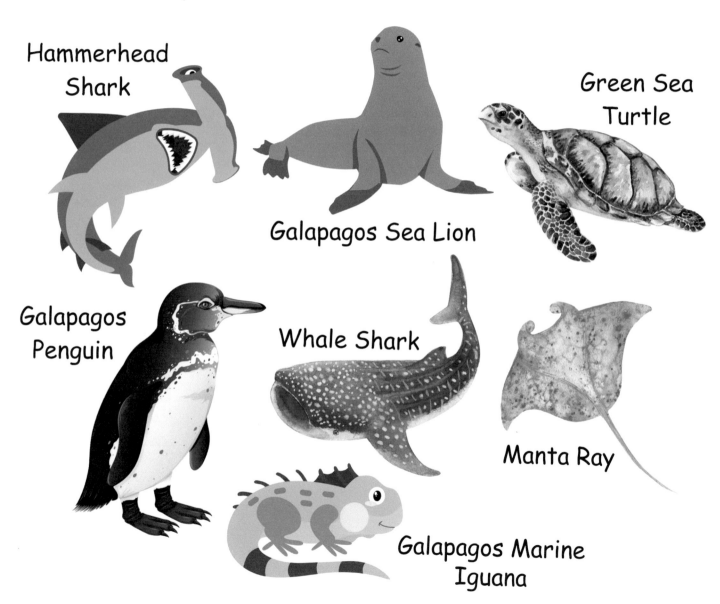

Hammerhead Shark

Galapagos Sea Lion

Green Sea Turtle

Galapagos Penguin

Whale Shark

Manta Ray

Galapagos Marine Iguana

WILD LIFE

Eco system most diverse in the world

Jaguar

Poison Dart Frog

Giant Otter

Spectacled Bear

Howler Monkey

Tapir

Ocelot

Harpy Eagle

Anaconda

SPORTS & ADVENTURES

Popular Sports are as follows

Football (Soccer)

Hiking

Zip lining

Surfing

Snorkeling

Rafting

BIRDS & BUTTERFLY

Paradise for birds watchers

1663 Species

4000 Butterfly varierty

FAMOUS PEOPLE

Juan Montalvo
(writer)

Oswaldo Guayasamín
(artist)

Eloy Alfaro
(revolutionary
leader)

Jaime Nebot
(politician)

ARTS & CRAFTS

Pottery

Woven textiles

Panama hats

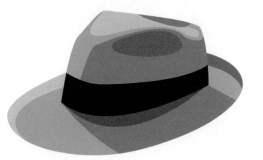

Wood carvings

Silver jewelry

CUISINE

Country has multi cultural society

Ceviche

Llapingachos

Seco de Pollo

Encebollado

Fanesca

Empanadas

Arroz con Pollo

Tigrillo

Bolón de Verde

Locro de Papa

Hornado

Mote Pillo

FESTIVALS

Inti Raymi
(Sun Festival)

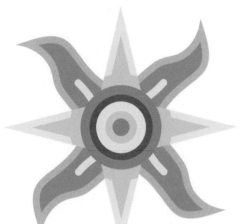

Carnival

Day of the
Dead

Mama
Negra

Fiesta de la Fruta y de
las Flores

UNESCO- WORLD HERITAGE SITES

Galapagos Islands

City of Quito

Sangay National Park

Historic Center
of Cuenca

Qhapaq Ñan, Andean
Road System

MUSIC INSTRUMENTS

Charango

Andean flute
(quena)

Marimba

Guitar

Drum

INTERNATIONAL RELATIONS

United Nations

The Organization of American States.

- Ecuador maintains diplomatic relations with various countries, particularly within Latin America, and is a member of international organizations such as the United Nations and the Organization of American States.

FUN FACTS

- Ecuador is named after the equator, which runs through the country.

- It is one of the most biodiverse countries in the world.

- The Andes Mountains

- Its run through Ecuador, offering stunning landscapes and adventure opportunities.

- The volcanoes

- It has the highest active volcano in the world, Cotopaxi.

- There are 27 active volcanoes in Ecuador.

- The panama hat

- The Panama hat actually originated in Ecuador, not Panama.

- The Plants

- There are more than 25,000 species of plants in Ecuador.

- The Galapagos tortoise

- It is the largest living species of tortoise and can live for over 100 years.

- The canelazo

- Ecuador's national drink is called "canelazo," a warm, spiced drink made with aguardiente (sugar cane alcohol), water, cinnamon, and sugar.

- The National dance.

- Ecuador's national dance is the "pasillo," a slow, romantic dance that originated in the Andes region.

- The city of Baños is known as the "Gateway to the Amazon".

- Its famous for its hot springs and adventure sports like rafting and ziplining.

- Ecuador's national flower is the rose, and the country is famous for its high-quality roses, which are exported all over the world.

- The Quilotoa crater lake is a popular tourist destination in Ecuador, known for its stunning turquoise waters.

- The Provinces

- Ecuador has 24 provinces, each with its own unique culture and traditions.

- The traditional Ecuadorian dish, ceviche, is made with raw fish marinated in citrus juices and is served with onions, tomatoes, and cilantro.

- The Galapagos Islands, part of Ecuador, inspired Charles Darwin's theory of evolution.

Made in the USA
Columbia, SC
09 December 2024

48880837R00024